MFM2P Revision Guide

Essential Skills for Grade 10 Mathematics in Ontario

By Mark Burke © 2012

ISBN : 147837828X

Written with the help of students at Astolot Educational Centre, Ottawa.

How to use this booklet

This booklet was written primarily to reinforce an understanding of the basics of the Ontario module MFM2P, Applied Mathematics grade 10. However GCSE, IGCSE and other international students may find much of the material useful too. It is aimed at those students who have usually found mathematics difficult and are looking for help getting to a C or B grade or Level 3. Once they have a strong grasp of the essentials, they can then look to moving up to grade 'A' level. Since the booklet is focused on grasping the basics and passing the module, those students looking for an 'A' grade should use it as a foundation for their study, but are also advised to look at more extension material and practice exams to be sure of achieving a Level 4. Where Level 4 students may find this booklet useful is in clearing up misconceptions about particular topic areas.

Because the booklet is designed to be short and affordable for all, by its' nature it has a limited number of exercises and is not intended to be a complete textbook. Ultimately mathematics requires plenty of practice and repetition for complete mastery, and mathematics students should always look to practice skills in different contexts using as many different sources as possible. *Nonetheless, this booklet has covered all the specific expectations as outlined in the Ministry of Education publication 'The Ontario Curriculum, Grade 9 and 10 : Mathematics' (2005).* Students who can successfully work through the exercises and examples here can be confident of having grasped the essential skills that should guarantee a passing grade at least, and I believe a Level 3.

Each topic section contains an example, and then a brief exercise in which students can test themselves under the '*NOW YOU TRY:*' sections. Answers are at the back. Students should *work* through the examples too, as opposed to just reading through them.

Please note diagrams are not to scale.

Mark Burke, August 2012

2

CONTENTS

3

Section A : MEASUREMENT AND TRIGONOMETRY

The Metric System

-The metric system is based on tens and multiples of ten with standard prefixes, so most conversions can be done *by moving a decimal point or adding zeroes.*
-For example, with grams we have milli grams (a thousand*th* of a gram) and kilograms (one thousand grams).

E.g - To convert 4.23 grams into milligrams, *multiply* by a 1000, or move the decimal 3 places *right* (milligrams are *smaller* , so there are *more* of them) :
4.23 x 1000 = 4230 milligrams.

E.g 2 - To convert 1600 metres into kilometres, *divide* by 1000 or move the decimal *left* (kilometres are larger so there are fewer of them):
16000m / 1000 = 1.6 kilometres

Know the following prefixes which tell you if something is ten times smaller/larger or some multiple of :

Giga = 1 000 000 000
Mega = 1 000 000
Kilo = 1000
hecto = 100
deka = 10
deci = 0.1
centi = 0.01
m1 = 0.001
micro- µ (mu) = 0.000 001

NOW YOU TRY 1:   : i) *Convert 0.459 Litres into millilitres*
ii)   *Convert 330 millilitre into Litres*
iii)   *Convert 500 megabytes into gigabytes*

4

Metric / Imperial Conversions

Below are some of the most useful and common conversions between metric and imperial (they are not all exact). To get from the right to left, divide instead of multiply, e.g :
1 mile = 1. 6 km, so 8 miles = 8 x 1.6 = 12.8 km.
To get from km back to miles, *divide* by 1.6

Other conversions (many approximate):
1 inch   = 2.54 cm
12 inches   = 1 foot
3 feet   = 1 yard
1 kilogram   = 2.23 pounds (lbs)
1 fluid ounce (oz.)   = 29 ml
1 cup   = 240 ml
1 pint   = 568 ml
Farenheit   = 1.8 C + 32
Celsius   = (F – 32) / 1.8

Some Common Imperial conversions : 1 yd = 3 ft
                                               1 ft = 12 inches
                                               1 gallon = 8 pints

example conversion : How many litres are in a gallon (eg, for comparing petrol gas prices) ? 1 gallon = 8 pints
                                               = 8 x 568 ml
                                               = 4544 ml
                                               = 4.544 Litres

NOW YOU TRY 2 :   *i) Convert 180 cm into feet and inches*
ii)   Convert 220 lbs into Kg
iii)   Convert 3 litres into fluid ounces (oz)
iv)   Convert 95 farenheit to celsius
v)   Convert 20 km into miles

Similar Triangles and Congruency

-*Similar* triangles are triangles that are larger or smaller versions of each other that have the same *angles* and same *ratios* of sides.
 -*Congruent* triangles have exactly the same angles *AND* size.

5

eg. 1:
The triangle that has sides 3, 4 and 5 cm is a smaller *but similar* triangle to that which has sides 6, 8 and 10 cm (*all* sides on the larger triangle are twice as big)

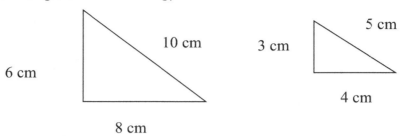

6 cm   10 cm   3 cm   5 cm

8 cm   4 cm

eg. 2 – Triangles which have *all* the same angles inside are similar, regardless of size.

We will now see how we can know with less information, but it is important that *corresponding* sides are similar for the triangle to qualify.

<u>Finding corresponding sides if triangles are similar</u>

If you have 3 out of 4 corresponding sides then you can use ratios to find the missing side. For example if a triangle has height 3cm and width 4cm, and a similar triangle has height 5cm and width 'x' , you can set up a ratio :
 $3/4 = 5/x$

$(3/4) x = 5$ (multiply both sides by x ; x cancels on the right side)
   $x = 5 \ / \ (\ 3/4)$ (divide both sides by ¾, ;
   $x = 20/3$ (dividing by ¾ is the same as multiplying by 4/3)
   $x = 6.67$ cm

NOW YOU TRY 3 :   *i) A triangle has hypotenuse 7m and height 4m. Another triangle has hypotenuse 20 m and height 11.4m . Are they similar, and how would you prove it ?*
ii)   A triangle has width 5m and height 6m. A similar triangle has height 10m. What is the width of the larger triangle ?

6

The Pythagorean Theorem

i) In a right triangle, the two short sides squared and then added equal the longest side squared. You can then square root this sum to find the long side.

eg. - If a triangle has short sides 8cm and 6cm, then the long side opposite the hypotenuse can be found using $8^2 + 6^2 = 64 + 36$ (make sure you square the numbers *before* you add them ; remember BEDMAS !)

$64 + 36 = 100$
$\sqrt{100} = 10$; the long side is 10cm.

6 cm

X cm

8 cm

ii) You can re-arrange the formula $a^2 + b^2 = c^2$ *to find short sides*.

The formula can be rewritten as $c^2 - a^2 = b^2$, or long side squared *minus* short side squared gives the other short side squared.

e.g : A triangle has hypotenuse 15 cm and width 9cm.
The missing side can be found with $15^2 - 9^2 = 225 - 81$
$225 - 81 = 169$
$\sqrt{169} = 13$ cm

NOW YOU TRY 4: i) *A right triangle has width and height 3m and 6m respectively. Find the length of the hypotenuse*
ii) *A right triangle has hypotenuse 8cm and height 7cm. Find the width.*
iii) *A right triangle has hypotenuse 11m and width 9m. Find the height.*

Trigonometry (in Right triangles) using Sine (Sin.) , Cosine (Cos.) and Tangent (Tan.) ratios

-There are 3 formulae that can be used to find angles inside right triangles, and find lengths if given an angle and one other length.
-They can be remembered as **'SOHCAHTOA'** (*'Saw-Ka-Toe-Ah'*)
Where **s**in x = **o**pposite/ **h**ypotenuse, **c**os x = adjacent/ hypotenuse, and tan x = opposite / adjacent .

First of all, you must understand that although the hypotenuse is always the same in a right triangle (longest side, opposite the right angle), *the adjacent and opposite can change depending on what angle you are working with.*

In the two congruent triangles below, the adjacent and opposite switch around depending on whether you use angle 'x' or angle 'y'. An easy way to remember this is that the adjacent is always the shorter side touching the angle, whilst the opposite is literally across from the angle.

Finding angles if given two sides

-First label the sides of the triangle according to which angle you are trying to find.
E.g in this case the sides from angle 'x' are hypotenuse and adjacent.

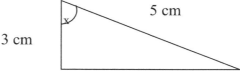

3 cm

-Next choose the appropriate formula ; in this case cos x = adjacent/ hypotenuse.

– 	Write out the ratio, and use the inverse/ shift function on your calculator on that ratio. In this case :

Cos x° = 3/ 5
cos $^{-1}$ (3/ 5) = 53.1 °

8

Finding a side if given an angle and another side

As before, write out the ratio based on what sides are involved *relative to the angle*.

e.g. In this case because we have the adjacent and we are looking for the opposite (relative to the angle) , we use the tan rat o :

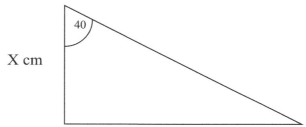

X cm

tan 40° = adj. / 6cm

tan 40° x 6 = adjacent
            x = 5cm

6 cm

- Beware of getting the ratio the right way up and the trickier algebra if the side you are looking for is on the denominator. Eg.2 ;

In this triangle we have the opposite and need the hypotenuse, so we use Sine.

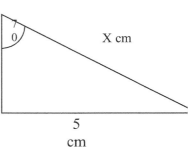

X cm

Sin 70° = 5cm / hyp.

Sin 70° x hyp. = 5cm

hypotenuse = 5cm / (Sin 70°) = 5.3 cm

5 cm

NOW YOU TRY 5: i) Calculate the angle x.

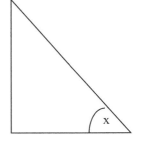

5 cm

x

9

3 cm

ii) Calculate the side x

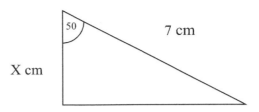

50

7 cm

X cm

Surface Area and Volume using metric/imperial conversions

Most of these problems involve 3-D shapes. Think of volume as how many slices you have of a shape, and surface area as the area of the outside faces only. You will often have to apply trigonometry to these problems.

Eg. 1 – Surface area and volume of a simple rectangular prism that measures 3cm (height) by 4cm (length) by 5cm (width).

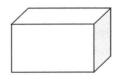

⊦ cm

The surface area is the total of the faces.
Note there are two of each face, e.g front and back are the same, the sides are the same, and the top and bottom are equal too.

S.A = 2 [(l x w) + (l x h) + (w x h)]
S.A = 2 [(4 x 5) + (4 x 3) + (5 x 3)]
S.A = 2 [20 + 12 + 15] = 2 x 47
S.A = 94cm².

The volume can be found simply using V = l x w x h
 or V = 5 x 4 x 3 = 60cm³.
It is also useful to think of taking a 'slice' of the shape and multiplying by the 3rd dimension. The area of the front face is 3 x 5 = 15cm². Now multiply by 4cm, or imagine 4 slices through the shape. V = 4 x 15cm = 60cm³.

10

<u>Cylinders</u> involve a slightly different formula but the idea of multiplying by slices is the same. Look at a cylinder of diameter 8 cm and height 6cm.

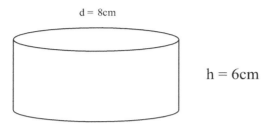

d = 8cm

h = 6cm

Find the area of the circle top or bottom using pi x r².
In this case A = 3.142 x 4² = 157.95 cm²
Multiply this answer by the height 6 cm to find volume :
 V = 6 x 157.95 = 947.73 cm³ (*Note * : I have rounded answers to 2 d.p to save space, but you should only round FINAL answers. Use the 'Ans' button on your calculator to use previous answers and retain accuracy.*)

<u>To find surface area of a cylinder</u> use the circumference times the height to find the 'wrap around' section (if you peel a label off a can you will see this is height x length where length = circumference).
In this case the curved surface area is 6cm x 3.142 x 8 = 150.816 cm²

<u>Volume of cones</u> :, Cones are just one third of a regular prism that has the same height and width.
E.g A cone has one third the volume of a cylinder that has the same dimensions. So just use the cylinder formula then divide by 3.

<u>Surface area of a cone</u> *uses the slant length instead of height,* and you may need to use Pythagoras with the height to calculate slant length.
Imagine a Right Triangle slice sitting inside the cone.
Slant length is then used to calculate the curved part of the cone using
Curved area = pi x r x S.

In this cone the slant length can be found using the radius as the base.
$S^2 = h^2 + r^2$, in this case $S^2 = 4^2 + 2.5^2 = 4.72$ cm

h = 4 cm

h = 4cm   S

R = 2.5 cm

d = 5cm

Slant length (S) is now used in the surface area formula : S.A = pi x r² (for the circle base)   + (pi x r x S).
S.A = (3.142 x 2.5²) + (3.142 x 2.5 x 4.72) = 56.71 cm ²

A pyramid uses the same principle as a cone for volume ; just find one third the volume of a regular prism that has the same dimensions.

The surface area of a pyramid involves finding the slant length which is used as the 'height' of a face. *In this case slant length means the line which runs down the middle of each face.*
Like a cone, use Pythagoras with half the width to find slant length.
In this case use height 5cm with width 6cm : $S^2 = 5^2 + 3^2$; S = √ 34 = 5.83cm
Once you found the slant length use it as the height of each face.
In this case the area of each face is   A = √ 34 x 6 = 35cm.
The total area of a square based pyramid is the base plus 4 times the face area.
S. A = (6 x 6) + 4 (√ 34 x 6) = 175.94 cm²

6cm

For balls or Spheres use S.A = 4 x 3.142 x r^2 (think of 4 circles)
For volume of spheres use V = 4/3 x 3.142 x r^3 (remember the 3's are in the volume formula)

Sample Mixed problem : A cone has a height of 16 cm and diameter 10 cm. What is the surface area in square inches ?

- We need slant length, which is $S^2 = 16^2 + 5^2$; S = 16.76 cm
  S.A in cm is : S.A = (3.142 x 5^2) + (3.142 x 5 x 16.76)
  = 341.90cm². Since 2.5 cm = 1 inch, 341.90/2.5 = approx. 137 inches

  NOW YOU TRY 6: I) *A swimming pool measures 8 feet by 4 feet by 20 feet. What is the volume of water it can hold in litres ?*

iii) *A basketball has a diameter of 28cm. What is it's surface area in cm, and how much air can it hold in litres ?*

iv) *A cardboard pyramid has a square base of 5cm by 5cm. Each face has a slant length of 7cm. Find the volume of the pyramid.*

Section B : Modelling Linear Relations (y = mx + b)

Review : Algebraic manipulation and Linear Equations :

There is one golden rule of manipulating algebraic equations ; '
What you do to one side of the equation you must also do the
same to the other side'
Most of the time this involves reversing operations to isolate a
variable, and making sure you apply the reverse operation to
both sides.

For example, rearrange the equation below so that 'y' is the
subject (y = ...)

$4x - 3y = 12$

$- 3y = 12 - 4x$ (subtract '4x' from both sides to start isolating
'y').

$y = (12 - 4x)/ (- 3)$ (divide both sides by -3 to get one single,
positive y)

$y = 4 + (4/3)x$ (*every* part of the equation on the left is divided
by 3)

Most basic equations involve these two basic steps ; using an
additive inverse and a multiplicative inverse.

This method can also apply to solving basic equations. You may
also have to collect like terms together before applying the
multiplicative inverse.

For example ; solve : $3x - 6 = 6x + 9$
 Try collecting the x's on the left side, and constants (plain
numbers) on the right

$3x - 6x = 9 + 6$ (note how the numbers that moved changed
signs +/-)
$-3x = 15$
$x = 15/ -3 = - 5$

14

Some of the trickier problems involve fractions which you can cancel by multiplying by the denominator of the fraction. For example, solve :

(1/3)x + 5 = 7

(1/3)x = 2

3 (1/3) x = 2 x 3   (cancel the 1/3 by multiplying by 3)
x = 6

NOW YOU TRY 7 :   i) *Solve for x :   3x – 4 = 18 + 5x*

ii) *Rearrange to make 'y' the subject :   5y – 3 = 4x + 8*

Graphing Relations

Linear Equations (equations involving 'x' to the power of 1 only) can be plotted on a graph as straight lines. A table of values is useful to record x values (horizontal moves on the graph) and the corresponding y values that pair with them (vertical movement on the graph)

For example, to plot the equation y = 3x – 4 on a graph :

Pick an 'x' value (any will do, but you want something near the origin 0,0 so x = 0 is a good start.
Substitute your x value into the equation.
If y = 3x – 4, then if x = 0

y = 3 (0) - 4 = - 4.

x= 0, y = - 4 can be written as an ordered pair', or co-ordinate on a graph. (from the middle, do not move left or right as x = 0, but as y = - 4, go up – 4.)

Repeat the procedure with another x value, eg. Pick x = 1 and sub into y = 3x – 4
If x = 1 , y = 3 (1) – 4 = -1
So we have the point (1, -1) to plot.

15

Now that you have two points you can join them up and extend a line. This is the line of the equation.

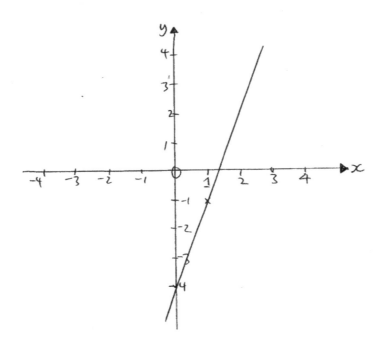

NOW YOU TRY 8: i) *Plot the equation* $3x - y = 5$ *as a line on a graph*

Y = mx + b : the general equation of a line

When plotting equations, you can find the gradient or **slope of a line** by looking at the number in front of x *if the equation is in the form y = mx + b.*

In the above example, if y = <u>3</u>x - 4, then the slope is +<u>3</u>. For every one unit you go across, you go up 3 units.

If an equation is not in the form y = mx + b then you can rearrange it so it is.

16

E.g if given $2y - 4x = 6$, rearrange for y :

$2y = 6 + 4x$
$y = 3 + \underline{2}x$. Now you can tell that the slope is 2 (the number if front of x).

The general equation of a line also tells you the y-intercept ; the point at which the line crosses the vertical axis. In the equation this is the constant ; that is the number on it's own
 In the equation $y = 3x - 4$, the y-intercept is - 4.

NOW YOU TRY 9:   _Find the slope and y-intercept : i) 2y + 7 = x   ii) 1/2 y - x = 4_

Finding intersections of lines using graphical and algebraic methods

a) <u>Graphical Method</u> :

Plot each equation by using a table of values or other

e.g : Solve i) y = 3x + 1 , and ii) y = 2x – 4.

For y = 3x +1 , try x = 0 ;

- If x = 0, y = 3 (0) + 1 = 1. So we have the point (0, 1).

Repeat for another x-value of y = 3x + 1 :

- If x = 1, y = 3 (1) + 1 = 4. Hence we have the point (1, 4).

Plot both these points and join them up to draw the line of y = 3x +1.

It should look like the diagram below.

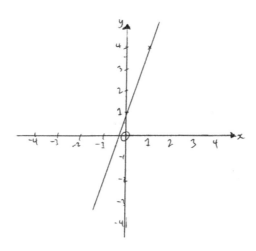

For y = 2x – 4, first try x = 0 :

If x = 0 , y = 2(0) - 4 = -4. So we have the point (0, - 4).

If x = 1, y = 2 (1) – 4 = -2. So we have the second point (1, -2)

- Plot this line on the same graph :

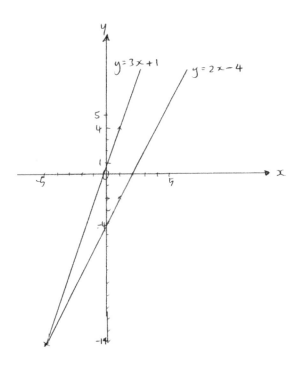

The solution is where the 2 lines intersect ; in this case (-5, -14).

At this particular point both equations have the same x and y values.

NOW YOU TRY 10 :

Find the intersection of y = 3x – 1 and y = - 4x + 2

b) Algebraic Substitution:

If the equations are not in the form y = mx + b , it may be more convenient to rearrange one of them and sub it in to the other equation.

e.g i) x + y = 3 and ii) 2y +4x = 7.

It's easiest to rearrange (i) ; If x + y = 3, then y= 3 – x

Replace 'y' in the second equation with '3 -x '.

   ii.   2 (3 - x) + 4x = 7

        6 – 2x + 4x = 7

        2x = 7 – 6

        x = 1/2

Now take the first solution and sub it in to the first equation :

   i.   If y = 3 – x,

        y = 3 – 1/2

        y = 2½

The solution is (1/2, 2½)

NOW YOU TRY 11: Solve x + y = 8 and x = 3y + 4

c)   Algebraic Elimination :

Sometimes equations can be lined up and added or subtracted to eliminate a variable. It may be necessary to multiply both equations by a number to get the same number of a certain variable. You want the same number of x's or y's in both equations, so that when you add or subtract equations one of the variables does actually get eliminated.

eg.

For the equations i) $2x - 3y = -6$ and ii) $3x - 5y = -11$

Multiply the first equation by 3, and the second equation by 2, so you have $6x$ in both equations. Note that everything must be multiplied by the 2 and 3.

x3 i) $6x - 9y = -18$

x2 ii) $6x - 10y = -22$

Because we have 6x in both equations we can subtract one from the other to eliminate x and solve for y :

$$i) - ii) : (6x - 6x) + (-9y - - 10y) = -18 - - 22$$

$$0 - 9y + 10y = -18 + 22$$

$$y = 4$$

Now go back to one of the *original* equations and solve for the other variable.

If $y = 4$, i) $2x - 3(4) = -6$

$2x - 12 = -6$

$2x = 6$

$x = 3$. The full solution is (3, 4).

d) Application to Word Problems

In most of these problems, x and y represent quantities of a variable and will be expressed as ;

   i.   x + y = total quantity
   ii.   x (cost of 1 x) + y (cost of 1y) = total cost

e.g. A large group of people buy tickets at a cinema. A total of 32 tickets are bought ; a mix of adult and child tickets. Child tickets cost 8 dollars, and adult tickets 10 dollars. The total cost of all the tickets comes to 280 dollars. How many of each type of ticket were bought ?

Equation 1 expresses the total quantity : i) x + y = 32

Equation 2 shows total cost : ii) 8x + 10 y = 280

This can now be solved using a method of your choice.

NOW YOU TRY 12 : *Solve the above problem*

Section C : Quadratic Relations of the form y = ax² + bx + c

Expanding and simplifying second degree polynomials : When you have two bracketed terms times each other, you must multiply everything in the second bracket by the first term in the first bracket, then all of the second bracket by the next term in the second bracket   ; e.g.

$$(2x + 5) \times (3x - 4) = (2x)(3x) - 2x(4) + 5(3x) - 5(4)$$
$$= 6x^2 - 8x + 15x - 20$$
$$= 6x^2 + 7x - 20 \quad (\text{collect and simplify}$$
like terms).

Or you can present it slightly differently :

e.g 2 : $(x + 3)^2 = (x + 3)(x + 3)$
$$= x(x + 3) + 3(x + 3)$$
$$= x^2 + 3x + 3x + 9$$
$$= x^2 + 6x + 9$$

*Note how $(x + 3)^2$ does NOT equal $x^2 + 3^2$!

NOW YOU TRY 13 : Expand and simplify $(2x - 9)^2$

Factorising Binomials and trinomials

To factor a polynomial you need to find common factors and remove them by division. It is the reverse of expanding brackets.

In the example below, both a 6 and an 'x' can be divided out of each term :

$$36x^2 - 18x = 6x(6x - 3)$$

Both terms have been divided by 6x and the result put in brackets. Note how you can check your answer by expanding the brackets ;

23

$6x (6x - 3) = (6x) (6x) + 6x (-3) = 36x^2 - 18x$

NOW YOU TRY 14 : *Factorise : i) 8x² - 70 x⁴ ii)   3x
− 9x² + 27x³*

The Difference of Two Squares is a unique method used
when a polynomial can be written as one number squared
minus another number squared . It uses the fact that (a
− b) (a + b) = a² - b² (middle terms cancel because a²
- ab + ab - b² = a² - b²
e.g
 x² - 25 can be written as (x)² - (5)²

(x)² - (5)² = (x − 5) (x + 5)

e.g 2:   9y² - 64x² = (3y − 8x) (3y + 8x)

 NOW YOU TRY 15 : *i)   4x² - 16y²   ii) 9x² + 100y²*

Factorising trinomials of the form ax² +bx + c

After trying common factors, and difference of two squares, some
trinomials can be factorised nonetheless into two sets of
brackets.
The method uses factors of the end term that also add to make
the middle term.
In the trinomial   x² + 5x + 6, the factors of 6 are 6 and 1, or 2
and 3. 2 and 3 also add to make 5 (the coefficient of the middle
term) so we can factorise our trinomial as (x + 2) (x + 3)

In the trinomial   x² - 4x − 12 we have the factors of - 12 as ; (-1,
12) (-2,6) (-3, 4) or (1, -12) (2, -6) (3, - 4) . Now looking at -
4x, we need the pair of factors that adds to make - 4.
Only 2 and - 6 will work (in that they both add to -4 AND multiply
to -12) so our factorisation is :   (x +2) (x − 6)

NOW YOU TRY 16 : *Factorise : i) x² - 3x − 40 (ii) x² + 5x − 14
(iii) x² - 8x + 12*

24

Graphing Quadratic Equations

The graph $y = x^2$ looks like :

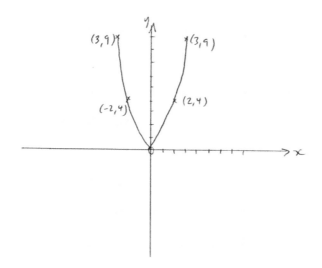

We will be looking at variations of this basic graph.

Note that we will not work with a table of values and will 'sketch' graphs instead of plotting them.
When a quadratic equation is factorised you can get a good idea of what the graph will look like. All quadratics when graphed have a curve shape called a parabola. $y = +x^2$ look like :

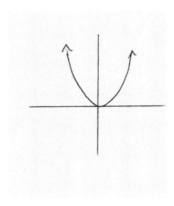

and $y = -x^2$ looks like :

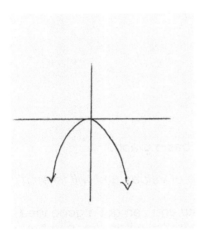

Like the line $y = mx + b$, the constant tells you where the graph cuts the y-axis.
- In the equation $y = x^2 - 4x - 5$, we know the curve has a y –intercept of -5.

We can also factorise this curve to get the x-intercepts :

$x^2 - 4x - 5 = (x - 5) (x + 1)$. The *x-intercepts or 'zeroes'* are when y = 0. Since zero times anything is zero, we can use values that bring either bracket to zero.
If $x - 5 = 0$, then x = 5. And if x + 1 = 0, then x = -1.

Parabolas are also symmetrical around a mirror line called *the*

26

axis of symmetry. If you have x-intercepts you can find this axis of symmetry *halfway* between them. The gap between 5 and -1 is 6 units, so come in 3 from either point and you will have the line x = 2.

Lastly you can find the bottom or top of the graph, called the *vertex.*
The vertex is the y- value that corresponds to the axis of symmetry. To find the vertex input the value from the axis of symmetry into the full equation.
In this case, if x =2, then y = (2)² - 4 (2) – 5 = - 9.

<u>To summarise , then :</u> In the above example, we know the curve
-opens upwards
-has x-intercepts 5 and -1
-a y-intercept of -5
-axis of symmetry line x = 2.
-It has a vertex of -9.
 Putting it altogether makes a graph that looks roughly like :

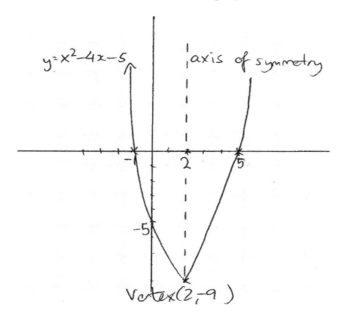

<u>NOW YOU TRY 17 :</u> *Use factorisation to help you sketch the*

curve $y = x^2 - 3x - 10$, showing clearly the y and x intercepts, the axis of symmetry and the vertex.

Vertex Form :
Quadratic Equations are often written in 'vertex form' $y = a (x - h)^2 + k$.
This allows the vertex to be located immediately as (h, k). This is particularly useful when a graph is above or below the x-axis and does not have x-intercepts.

e.g. In the equation $y = 3 (x + 8)^2 + 20$ the vertex is (-8, 20).
Note that you also have the axis of symmetry as x = - 8.
Be careful to note that in vertex form the constant is NOT the y-intercept.
If we expanded our vertex equation to standard form, we would have :
$y = 3 (x^2 + 16x + 64) + 20$
$= 3x^2 + 48x + 172 + 20$
$= 3x^2 + 48x + 192$ (the y-intercept is 192).

A graphical check confirms :

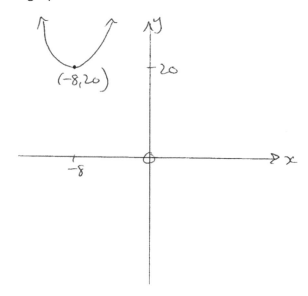

Application of Quadratic Graphs to Real Life Problems :

28

Most of these problems involve the flight of an object where the x-axis is time and the y-axis is height. E.g :
 A baseball is thrown and it's flight modelled with the parabola
 $h = -\frac{1}{2}(t^2 - 3t - 4)$, where h is height in metres and t = time in seconds.
 Find the maximum height the ball reaches and the time when the ball hits the ground.
The $-\frac{1}{2}$ will not affect x-intercepts so we can factorise the bracketed term :
$h = -\frac{1}{2} (t - 4) (t + 1)$.
If the zeroes are t =4 and t =-1, then we have a vertex at t = 2.5 .
If t = 2.5, then $h = -\frac{1}{2} (2.5 - 4) (2.5 + 1) = 2.625m$
2.625 metres is in fact the maximum height the ball reaches.
Our ntercept t = 4 is the moment when the ball hits the ground.
 Note that since this is a real world problem we disregard the other x- intercept t = -1 .

NOW YOU TRY 18: A divers jump is tracked and analysed by a computer, which uses the vertex equation $h = - (t - 2.5)^2 +8.75$ to model the trajectory of the dive. Use the equation to find :
i) the maximum height the diver reaches, and ii) the time at which the diver hits the surface.

MFM2P Answer Sheet:

CHECK YOUR ANSWERS 1 *:   i) 0.459 x 1000 = 459 ml   ii)*
330/1000 =330 litres   iii) 50/1000 = 0.5 gigs

CHECK YOUR ANSWERS 2 *: i) 180 /2.54 = 71 inches = 5 feet*
11 inches = 5' 11"   ii) 220 / 2.23 = 97 kg   iii) 3000/29 = 103 oz

iv)   (95 – 32)/1.8 = 35°C   v) 20/1.6 = 12.5 miles

CHECK YOUR ANSWERS 3: i)   yes, ratio of hypotenuse to
height in both triangles is 1.75 , or the sides on the larger triangle
are approx. 2.86 times bigger   ii) 5x (10/6) = 8.33m

CHECK YOUR ANSWERS 4 : i) $3^2 + 6^2 = 45$; hyp. = 6.7 m   ii)
$8^2 - 7^2 = 15$cm ; width = 3.9cm   iii) $11^2 - 9^2 = 40$; height =6.3 m

CHECK YOUR ANSWERS 5 : l) Tan x = 3/5 ; x = 31°   ii)
Cos50°= x/7 ; x = 4.5 cm

CHECK YOUR ANSWERS 6 : i) Convert feet to inches, then
cm. V= 243.84cm x 121.92cm x 609.6 cm = 18,122,781.82 cm^3 =
same in ml. 18,122,781.82 ml = 18,122.78 Litres ii) S.A : 4 x
3.142 x 14^2 = 2463 cm^2 . V = 4/3 x 3.142 x 14^3 = 11495.53ml =
11.496 Litres
iii) $7^2 - 2.5^2$ = 42.75 ; height = 6.54cm. V= 1/3 (5 x 5 x 6.54 cm)
= 54.5cm^3

CHECK YOUR ANSWERS 7 : i) 3x- 5x = 18 +4 ; 2x = 22 ; x =11
ii) 5y = 4x +11 ; y = (4/5)x + (11/5)

30

CHECK YOUR ANSWER 8 :

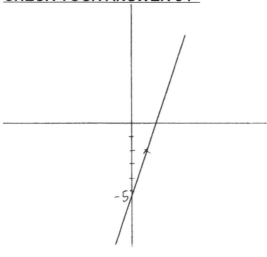

___

CHECK YOUR ANSWER 9 : *i) m = 1/2, intercept is -3.5 ii) m = 2, intercept is 8*

CHECK YOUR ANSWER 10 : 3x – 1 = - 4x +2 ; 7x = 3 ; solution (3/7. 2/7)

CHECK YOUR ANSWER 11 : *y = 8 –x ; x = 3 (8 - x) +4 ; solution (7 , 1)*

CHECK YOUR ANSWER 12 : x = 20, y = 12.

CHECK YOUR ANSWER 13 : 4x² - 36x + 81

CHECK YOUR ANSWER 14 : i) 2x² (4 – 35x²)   ii) 3x (1 – 3x + 9x²)

CHECK YOUR ANSWER 15 : i) (2x – 4y) (2x +4y) ii) does not factorise due to addition sign.

CHECK YOUR ANSWERS 16 : i) (x − 8) (x + 5) (ii) (x + 7) (x − 2) (iii)
(x − 2) (x + 6)

CHECK YOUR ANSWER 17 :

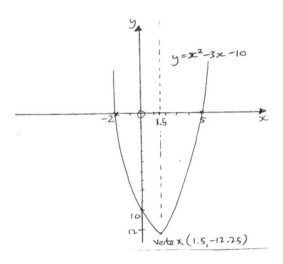

CHECK YOUR ANSWER 18 : i) vertex (2.5, 8.75) ii) 6
seconds.

32

CPSIA information can be obtained at www.ICGtesting.com
Printed in the USA
LVOW01s1955160915

454381LV00040BA/766/P